East of Eden

Living in the Shadow of the Garden:
A Study of Genesis 4:16

F. Wayne Mac Leod

Light To My Path Book Distribution
Sydney Mines, N.S CANADA B1V 1Y5
www.ltmp.ca

East of Eden

Copyright © 2014 by F. Wayne Mac Leod

A Special thanks to the proof readers:

Diane Mac Leod, Pat Schmidt

Table of Contents

PREFACE

This is a simple study of Genesis 4:16. When the Lord first put a burden on my heart to write on this verse I wasn't sure what I would find as I did not approach it with any particular objective in mind. As I took the time to reflect however, the Lord showed me its richness and application.

In many ways Cain's story in Genesis 4:16 is our story. It is the story of a man's rebellion and wandering from God. As we watch Cain leave the presence of God we become aware of our own temptations to wander. We recognize just how much we, too, struggle with the attractions of this world and our own sinful heart.

This passage, however, is more than the story of Cain's rebellion. It is a revelation of the heart of God for His people. We were created to live in Eden. While sin stripped us of the privilege of experiencing the fullness of the Garden, the Lord Jesus has restored this privilege through His death and resurrection on our behalf. The blessings and privileges of Eden are again available to all who will receive the forgiveness offered through the Lord Jesus.

Will we open our hearts to experience afresh what God intended for us from the beginning? Will we enter the presence of God and learn to delight in Him and in the reality of who He is? I trust that this brief study will enable each reader to examine his or her life afresh. My prayer is that it would stimulate us to live again in the joy of God's presence and in the place of His fullest blessing.

May God bless you as you embark on this study.

F. Wayne Mac Leod

1

INTRODUCTION AND

CONTEXT

> Then Cain went away from the presence of the Lord and settled in the land of Nod, east of Eden (Genesis 4:16)

As we begin our study of Genesis 4:16 it is of utmost importance that we give some consideration to the context. There have been a number of important events leading, up to this verse. Let's take a moment to examine them.

Cain was the son of Adam and Eve, the first people created by God. We know the story of Adam and Eve and how, because of sin, they were driven from the Garden of Eden. Cain was born after Adam and Eve had been expelled from the Garden. He was their first child. At the time that sin entered the world, everything was relatively new. The world, in which Cain was born, though under the curse of sin, had not yet seen the full impact of that curse later generations would see. Nations were not at war with each other. Pagan religions did not yet exist. The earth had not yet seen murder, rape or violence against another human being. As the first child of Adam and Eve, Cain would reveal to the world what the effects of sin would be on the generations to come.

Genesis 4 recounts the story of the birth of Abel, the second child of Adam and Eve, and younger brother to Cain. As they grew up, the boys took on different professions. Cain worked the ground and cultivated its fruits. Abel kept sheep. Both of these were noble professions.

The time came for them to bring an offering to the Lord. Cain, as a tiller of the soil, brought an offering of the "fruit of the ground". Abel, as a sheep farmer, brought a firstborn sheep from his flock. The boys brought what they had as offerings to the Lord. Both of these were legitimate offerings.

In Genesis 4:4-5, however, we read that God accepted the offering Abel brought, but rejected Cain's offering. We are not told how these boys came to understand this, but it was clear that Cain's offering had been rejected. There are various opinions as to why Cain's offering was not accepted by God. Some believe it was because of the type of offering he brought. Some believe that Cain should have brought an animal sacrifice like his brother. The problem with this interpretation is that God's people were also commanded to bring the first of their crop harvest to the Lord (see Exodus 23:19; Leviticus 2:14; 23:10). The fruit of the land was an acceptable offering to God. This leads us to believe that there was another reason for God's rejection of Cain's offering.

We may not have to look far for the answer. Listen to Genesis 4:5:

> 5 But for Cain and his offering he had no regard. So Cain was angry and his face fell

Notice that Genesis 4:5 tells us that God had no regard for both Cain and his offering. This tells us that the issue was not just with the offering but also with Cain. When Cain saw that the Lord had accepted Abel's offering but rejected his, he became "very angry" and his face fell. In fact, the matter became so serious that God spoke to Cain about his attitude, warning him that sin was crouching at his door with a desire for him. What does this tell us about Cain?

Cain's heart was ready soil for evil and sin to grow. The fact that he became "very angry" with his brother shows us that the heart of Cain was not right with God or his brother. When his offering was rejected, this should have given him reason to seek the Lord about the reason for the rejection. He could then have repented and been restored to fellowship.

After his offering, however, God warned Cain about sin crouching at his door. God looked into Cain's heart and saw sin like a dam ready to burst. God told him that he needed to take control of the sin lest it break out. Cain did not listen. In the very next verse, Cain rose up and killed his brother in a jealous rage and then lied to God about what had happened.

What do these events reveal to us about the heart of Cain? He came to God with a jealous and bitter heart. It was a heart that was not in tune with God or ready to listen to Him. It was a heart filled with sin and rebellion. It was a murderous heart. Could it be that God was not looking at the offerings at all? Perhaps He was looking at the hearts of these two brothers who came to Him that day. He may have rejected Cain and his offering based on his sinful attitude, jealousy and rebellion.

Cain's action that day, despite the warning of God, brought the curse of God on his life. In Genesis 4:11 we read that God cursed the ground he cultivated and told him that it would no longer yield abundantly to him. He also told him that he would be a fugitive and wanderer on the earth, unable to settle down in any one place. While God removed His blessing from Cain, His grace was still evident. God put some kind of mark on him to protect him against anyone who would seek to kill him. Cain would leave the region of Eden, find a wife and have a family. While God allowed him this privilege, he would live the rest of his life separated from his family, and "away from the presence of the Lord" (Genesis 4:16).

The context of Genesis 4:16 reveals the effect of sin on the life of Cain. He wrestled with thoughts of jealousy, rebellion and murder in his heart. God warned him through the rejection of his offering. God warned him personally by telling him that sin was crouching at his door, but Cain did not listen. Instead, he hardened his heart and submitted to his sinful impulses. The result was not only the death of his brother, but also a deep separation between himself and his God.

For Consideration:

- What was the effect of sin on the earth and particularly in the life of Cain? Do you see seeds of this in your own life?
- How important is the attitude of the heart as we come to God in worship?

- How does Cain demonstrate a lack of humility and willingness to listen to God and His warnings? How could Cain have acted differently?
- What do we learn here about sin and how it crouches at our door? How does God warn us about this sin today?
- What evidence is there of God's grace in Cain's life even though he suffered the consequences for his rebellion?
- Have you experienced the grace of God when you have failed Him? Explain.

For Prayer:

- Ask God to give you victory over the sin that crouches at your door with a desire for you? What particular sins crouch at your door?
- Ask God to break any rebellion in your heart that would keep you from walking in obedience to His purpose for your life.
- Ask God to cleanse your heart from any jealousy, bitterness or anger.
- Do you have a brother or sister you need to forgive? Ask God to break any sinful attitudes in your heart toward that brother or sister.

2

CAIN

Then Cain... (Genesis 4:16)

In the previous chapter we examined the context of Genesis 4:16. In this chapter we will take a look at Cain's name and its significance. We read in Genesis 4:1 how Cain, the first child of Adam and Eve, received his name:

> Now Adam knew Eve his wife, and she conceived and bore Cain saying, "I have gotten a man with the help of the Lord"

From Genesis 4:1 we catch a glimpse of why Eve called her first son "Cain." We are told in this verse that it was because she had "gotten a man with the help of the Lord." The key to understanding this comes from the Hebrew language itself. The word translated "gotten" in Genesis 4:1 is the Hebrew word "qanah." It literally means to procure, to acquire or to possess. The Hebrew name for Cain is "qayin". Notice the similarities between these two words. Eve called her son "qayin" because he was a "qanah" (possession) from the Lord.

There is likely a sense of motherly tenderness in this name. This child was a treasured "possession" given to Eve (Genesis 4:1). The young life that rested in her arms had been given to her by the God she had sinned against. He was an expression of the Lord's continued blessing on her life despite her rebellion in the Garden.

While Cain was Eve's possession, Eve recognized that he had come from God. She and her husband, Adam, had recently been banished from the Garden of Eden because of their sin. This Garden had been given to them as their possession as well. For a time they enjoyed its fruitfulness, but because of their sin it was taken from them. Eve likely understood that nothing truly belonged to her. Everything she had was God's. She was merely a caretaker of what He put in her hands.

Cain's name is significant. It shows us that he did not belong to himself. He was a possession of God, given as a gift to his mother and father to be nurtured and loved. As a possession of God, he was obligated to the one who owned him and gave him life.

Writing to the Corinthian church, the apostle Paul said this:

> Or do you not know that your body is the temple of the Holy Spirit within you, whom you have from God? You are not your own, for you were bought with a price. So glorify God in your body. (1 Corinthians 6:19-20)

Notice what the apostle told the Corinthians. He told them that they did not belong to themselves. Their bodies were the temples of the Holy Spirit. They had been bought by the Lord Jesus as His own possession.

As a possession of the Lord, God's people had an obligation toward the One who owned them. In 1 Corinthians 6:20 the apostle Paul told them that because their bodies were the possession of the Holy Spirit, they were to glorify God in that body.

Cain's name reminded him that he did not belong to himself. He belonged to someone else. There was a special obligation placed on him as the possession of God to walk in a way that glorified the name of his Lord and Master.

How easy it is for us to lose sight of the fact that as Christians, we belong to God. We can live our lives with very little concern about what God expects of us. Cain reminds us that we are God's possession. Are we ready to live with this reality always before us? Will we surrender our own pleasures to seek His will? Will we surrender our plans to walk in His?

In this world, people have asserted their independence and freedom. Attention has shifted from God to our own goals and purposes in life. Is it not interesting that the very first child born into this world bore in his name a reminder that He belonged to someone else? Is this not a reminder to us that we were created to be possessed by God? This is not a popular idea in our day but it is one we need to be reminded of again. Until we understand that we were created by God and for God we will never experience the fullness He has for us.

Paul reminded the Roman believers in Romans 11:36:

> For from Him and through Him and for Him are all things. To Him be the glory forever! Amen (NIV)

Writing to the Colossian church the apostle would say:

> He is the image of the invisible God, the firstborn of all creation. For by him all things were created, in heaven and on earth, visible and invisible, whether thrones or dominions or rulers or authorities—all things were created through him and for him. (Colossians 1:15-16)

Notice in these two passages that God is the creator of all things and all things were created *for* Him. This means that you and I were created for God. We were born for His glory and to serve His great overall purpose. If we are to live our life to the full, we must come to the understanding that we are the Lord's and that our greatest joy and fulfillment will only come in surrender to Him and His purpose. As a possession of God, Cain's greatest purpose in life was to bring honour to the one to whom he belonged. This must be our great purpose and delight as well.

For Consideration:

- Why did Eve call her first son Cain?
- What is the significance of the name Cain? What did this mean for him?
- What does it mean to belong to God? What obligations does this bring?
- What are the blessings of belonging to God?
- Take a moment to examine your life. Does how you live your life reveal that you "are not your own"? Are there areas of your life you need to surrender to the Lord God? What are they?

For Prayer:

- Thank the Lord that as His possession you can be assured of His care and provision.
- Ask the Lord to reveal any area of your life that you have not surrendered to Him.
- Ask the Lord to help you to live each day with the understanding that He is your Lord and that you belong to Him.

3

CAIN WENT AWAY

Then Cain went away ... (Genesis 4:16)

In the first chapter of this study we examined the background to Genesis 4:16. There we saw how Cain, in a fit of jealous anger, killed his brother, despite the warning of God that sin was crouching at his door. It would be easy to focus on the sin of murder in this passage, but this is not Cain's only sin.

Cain's sin began in his heart. Even before he brought his offering to the Lord, there was a seed of jealousy and anger dwelling in him. This is quite clear from the fact that his offering was rejected by God. God rejected his offering because it did not come from a heart that was right with Him.

The rejected offering was a warning from God. It showed Cain that things were not right between him and his Creator. This should have humbled him and caused him to seek the Lord, but it didn't.

Throughout Scripture God often warned His people. In Amos 4:7 God did this by withholding rain:

> I also withheld the rain from you when there were yet three months to the harvest; I would send rain on one city, and send no rain on another city; one field would have rain, and the field on which it did not rain would wither.

In Hosea's day He spoke through the land and the animals:

> There is swearing, lying, murder, stealing, and committing adultery; they break all bounds, and bloodshed follows bloodshed. Therefore the land mourns, and all who dwell in it languish, and also the beasts of the field and the birds of the heavens, and even the fish of the sea are taken away. (Hosea 4:2-3)

The events detailed in Amos and Hosea were God's way of telling His people that something was not right. One city received the blessing of rain and the other city had none. One field would have rain and another field would wither. This should have caused the people of God to wonder what was going on. These warning were intended to cause God's to search their hearts.

In a similar way, the Lord God warned Cain by personally speaking to him. Listen to what the Lord told him in Genesis 4:6-7:

> The Lord said to Cain, "Why are you angry, and why has your face fallen? If you do well, will you not be accepted? And if you do not do well, sin is

crouching at the door, its desire is for you, but you must rule over it."

God made it clear to Cain that the reason his offering was not accepted was because he did not "do well". There was an obstacle he needed to overcome before his offering could be accepted. God warned him that sin was crouching at his door with a desire for him. The picture here is like a lion crouching down and ready to spring up at its prey. God told Cain that there was danger in the path he was treading. He warned him that a lion was ahead ready to spring out and overcome him.

Cain heard these warnings but instead of being humbled, he continued down the path he was taking. He gave into his anger and murdered his brother. He was guilty, not just of the sin of murder, but also of rejecting God and refusing to deal with the sin of his heart. Instead of confessing his sin, Cain chose to fan the flame and surrender to it.

When God asked Cain about his brother's whereabouts, Cain told Him he didn't know because he was not his brother's keeper (Genesis 4:9). Notice two things here. Notice first that Cain denies any obligation towards his brother and shows a total lack of concern for him. The words, "I am not my brother's keeper", indicate a distance between himself and his brother. Cain had allowed things to come between himself and Abel. Jesus would have something to say about this in Matthew 5:23-24:

> So if you are offering your gift at the altar and there remember that your brother has something against you, leave your gift there before the altar and go. First be reconciled to your brother, and then come and offer your gift.

Cain's sinful attitude toward his brother was a hindrance in his relationship with God. God held him responsible for this broken relationship.

We learn secondly from Genesis 4:9 that Cain lied to the Lord God. He told the Lord that he did not know where his brother was. There was a similar situation in Acts 5 when a man by the name of Ananias and his wife Sapphira sold a piece of property, kept part of the money for themselves and gave the rest to the church. They told the church, however, that they had given the full amount of the sale. The Holy Spirit revealed the lie to the apostle Peter who accused Ananias of lying to the Holy Spirit (Acts 5:3). As soon as he heard this accusation, Ananias fell down and died. His disrespect in lying to God brought a very serious punishment. His wife would suffer the same fate.

Not only did Cain allow things to come between himself and Abel but he also showed a tremendous disrespect for God by openly lying to Him. This disrespect led to the death of Ananias in the New Testament. It would not go unpunished in Cain's life.

As a result of Cain's rebellion and refusal to obey and humble himself, God cursed the land so that it would no longer "yield its strength" to him (Genesis 4:12). He told Cain that he would be a fugitive and wanderer on the earth. Cain's response to this punishment of God is interesting. Listen to what he said in Genesis 4:13-14:

> Cain said to the Lord, "My punishment is greater than I can bear. Behold, you have driven me today away from the ground, and from your face I shall be hidden, I shall be a fugitive and a

wanderer on the earth, and whoever finds me will kill me."

These verses again reveal something about Cain. Notice what he says here:

1. My punishment is greater than *I* can bear
2. You have driven *me* from the ground
3. Your face (blessings) shall be hidden from *me*
4. *I* shall be a fugitive and wanderer on the earth
5. Whoever finds *me* will kill *me*

Notice the repetition of the words "I" and "me". His concern here is for himself, the struggles he would have to face and the enemies he would have to deal with. He shows no sign of humbling himself before God. He is not moved to repentance by this judgement. Instead, his only response seems to be to complain about how difficult his life would be now that God had cursed him.

It is in this context that we see the next phrase of this verse—"Cain went away". This was a decision he made himself. The story is not unlike the story of Jonah, who did not want to go to Nineveh, and chose to board a boat heading in the opposite direction. The judgement of God did not move Cain to submission and surrender. His deepest regret was not that he broke fellowship with God or murdered his brother but that his life would be difficult now.

That day Cain "went away." This leaving was not just a matter of packing his bags and moving to another location. Leaving for Cain was much deeper than this. He left not only his family but also his relationship with God. He chose to wander. He chose to deny his faith and do things his own way. The "possession" of God now rebels against his Master and escapes to live life his own way. He turned his back on the blessing and fellowship of God to become the master of his own destiny.

This must have caused great grief to God, who watched him go. God did not stop Cain that day. Cain had made up his mind. He took the punishment of God and left for good, never to return. This phrase "Cain went away" ought to be a warning for us today. Maybe there are sins the Lord has been warning you about that you are not ready to deal with. Have we, by our persistent rebellion and refusal to listen to the warnings of God, made the same decision as Cain?

Cain went away. The treasured "possession" of God rebelled and chose his own way. He left the fellowship and blessing of God to follow his own path. He chose his pride over intimacy with God. He chose rebellion over surrender to His Lord. May the Lord give us tender hearts to heed His warnings. May He give us humble hearts to confess our sin so that we do not fall into the error of Cain.

For Consideration:

- What were Cain's sins?
- How did God warn Cain about his sin and the consequences? What was the response of Cain to those warnings?
- What evidence do we have that Cain's decision to walk away from God was of his own choosing?

- Do we have a free will? Can we choose to rebel against God like Cain? What are the consequences?
- Are there sins in your life the Lord has been warning you about today? What are they? What do you need to do about them?

For Prayer:

- Take a moment to confess your sin to the Lord. Ask Him to forgive you and give you a humble heart to walk in tune with Him.
- Ask the Lord to reveal anything that keeps you from a deeper fellowship with Him?
- If you have, like Cain, chosen to walk away from God, ask Him to forgive you and restore you to fellowship with Himself.
- Ask God to keep you from walking away from the fullness of His fellowship and blessing in your life.

4

THE PRESENCE OF THE LORD

Then Cain went away from the presence of the
Lord... (Genesis 4:16)

Notice as we continue this study of Genesis 4:16 that this
verse tells us that Cain went away from "the presence of
the Lord". Let's take a moment to consider this phrase.

King David reflected on this in Psalm 139:7-12 when he
said:

7 Where shall I go from your Spirit?
Or where shall I flee from your presence?
8 If I ascend to heaven, you are there!
If I make my bed in Sheol, you are there!
9 If I take the wings of the morning
and dwell in the uttermost part of the sea,
10 even there your hand will lead me,
and your right hand shall hold me.
11 If I say, "Surely the darkness shall cover me,
and the light about me be night,"
12 even the darkness is not dark to you;
the night is bright as the day,
for darkness is as light with you.

Notice in Psalm 139:7 how the psalmist uses the word "presence". This is the same Hebrew word used in Genesis 4:16. The Psalmist tells us, however, that he could not flee from the presence of God. Wherever he went, God was there watching over him. How are we to understand Genesis 4:16 in light of what Psalm 139:7-12 teaches? What did it mean for Cain to go away from the presence of the Lord?

This is not the only Old Testament verse that speaks about individuals seeking to withdraw from the presence of the Lord. Genesis 3:8 records how Adam and Eve hid from the presence of the Lord.

> And they heard the sound of the Lord God walking in the garden in the cool of the day, and the man and his wife hid themselves from the presence of the Lord God among the trees of the garden.

What is interesting in Genesis 3 is that while Adam and Eve hid themselves from the presence of the Lord among the trees, the Lord God engaged them in a conversation:

> But the Lord God called to the man and said to him, "Where are you?" And he said, "I heard the sound of you in the garden, and I was afraid, because I was naked, and I hid myself." (Genesis 3:9-10)

Obviously, they were not able to hide anywhere God could not find them. From the context of Genesis 3 we understand that Adam and Eve hid themselves out of shame over their nakedness. The response of Adam and Eve is a natural human response when experiencing shame. They were seeking to distance themselves from God out of fear and quilt.

The prophet Jonah too tried to flee from the presence of the Lord. We read in Jonah 1:3:

> But Jonah rose to flee to Tarshish from the presence of the Lord. He went down to Joppa and found a ship going to Tarshish. So he paid the fare and went down into it, to go with them to Tarshish, away from the presence of the Lord.

Jonah attempted to flee from the presence of the Lord. The reason for this was because God had called him to go to Nineveh and Jonah did not want to go. Again notice what happens as Jonah flees from the presence of the Lord.

> But the Lord hurled a great wind upon the sea, and there was a mighty tempest on the sea, so that the ship threatened to break up. (Jonah 1:5)

The story of Jonah is about the prophet seeking to flee from God and God pursuing him. Jonah could not get away from the presence of the Lord. Jonah's attempt to flee was a human response to his unwillingness to surrender to God's will. It was an attempt to distance himself somehow from God and His voice.

Perhaps you have been in a similar situation. Maybe you have been in a meeting where the Spirit of God was speaking powerfully to you about an area of sin in your life. As you sat in that meeting, the sense of the convicting presence of God began to increase in you. You were confronted with the need to make a decision -- either surrender to what God was saying or run away.

While you can never find a place where God will not find you, you feel the need to distance yourself from that voice of conviction.

There are many ways we can attempt to flee from the presence of the Lord. Adam and Even hid among the trees. Today we hide behind other things. I have met individuals who have become very busy in their work or social lives. Others hide among the pleasures of this world or in intellectual arguments. Still others surrender to addictions and lusts of all kinds. Behind all of these efforts is an attempt to distance themselves from God and the conviction of His Spirit.

Leaving the presence of the Lord is not so much about going where God cannot find me as much as it is about blocking any thought of God and His purpose from my mind, heart and attitude. This can be done in various ways. For Cain it meant leaving his parents and the faith they taught him.

How can anyone remain under the convicting presence of God if they are not ready to surrender to Him? We will do anything to get away from that conviction. I believe God would have forgiven a repentant Cain and restored him to fellowship but Cain was not ready for this. He chose another path—a path that blocked the presence of God from his heart and mind.

There are many such paths away from the presence of God. Some of these paths are religious in nature. Perhaps you have met individuals who have hidden themselves behind false doctrine to justify their sin. Maybe you have met individuals who bury themselves in Christian service feeling that if they are busy working for God they will not have to deal with God Himself. Some leave the fellowship of Christian believers because they do not want to deal with the constant reminder of their sin.

Cain went away from the presence of the Lord. This did not mean that he could go somewhere God could not find him. It was much deeper than this. Cain chose to block the Lord's presence from his life. He chose to fill his life with other things. He decided that God would no longer be his heart's delight and focus. He determined that he would live his own life. He would make his own decisions and do what he wanted. God would no longer be part of his agenda.

It is not an easy thing to live in the presence of the Lord. Those who live in His presence must bow to Him as Lord. This means that they must surrender to His purpose and plan for their lives. They must recognize that He is their Master and King and they are His servants. To live in the presence of the Lord is to realize that we must deal with sin that offends Him. This means that we must be willing to die to ourselves and our own ideas as obedience may place us in uncomfortable and difficult circumstances. For those who walk in His presence, however, the Lord promises fullness of joy (see Psalm 16:11). He also promises that even if we have to walk through the "valley of the shadow of death" He will be with us (see Psalm 23:4).

Cain made his decision. He chose to walk away from the presence of the Lord. He chose to close the door of his heart to the purpose of God His creator. God's treasured "possession" turned his back on Him and shut Him out of his life. May this not be your case today.

For Consideration:

- Can we go anywhere God cannot see or reach us?
- What is our human response when we are ashamed or have fallen into sin we do not want to renounce?
- What kind of things do we do to distance ourselves from the convicting and holy presence of God?
- Have you been seeking to flee from the presence of the Lord?
- What does it mean to live in the presence of God? What does this require of us? What are the blessings of being in His presence?

For Prayer:

- Thank the Lord that there is nowhere you can go where He does not see you or cannot reach you?
- Ask the Lord to soften your heart to His presence. Ask Him to give you a humble heart of obedience and submission.
- Ask the Lord to show you if there is any area of your life where you are resisting His convicting presence. Surrender this to Him today.
- Ask the Lord to reveal more of His presence to you and make you more willing to walk humbly in that presence.

5

SETTLING IN THE LAND OF NOD

> Then Cain went away from the presence of the Lord and settled in the land of Nod... (Genesis 4:16)

Genesis 4:16 goes on to tell us that, leaving the presence of God, Cain "settled in the land of Nod." The phrase "settled in the land of Nod" will be the focus of our attention here. There are some important details we need to see in the phrase.

Testimonies abound of men and women who, for a period of time, wandered from the truth and fellowship with God. They came to realize over time that they were not happy in their rebellion and repented of their sin and were restored to fellowship. This is the lesson of the prodigal son as recorded for us in the book of Luke. He left the presence and fellowship of his father to experience the world and its attractions. When he lost everything he had, he realized that he was better off with his father. He returned humbled and renewed in his zeal to remain with his father and live in fellowship with him.

In Genesis 13 we read the story of Abraham and Lot. The blessing of the Lord was so great in their lives that the land could not support the two families. Lot decided to leave Abraham and go to the region of Sodom and Gomorrah. Genesis 13:13 tells us something about the land Lot chose:

> Now the men of Sodom were wicked, great sinners against the Lord.

In choosing to leave Abraham, Lot was choosing to wander from God and His ways. He chose to bring his family to a region that was known for its wickedness and sin. Like Cain, he chose to leave the presence of the Lord. This decision proved to be very risky for Lot. Not only did he lose his wife to the attractions of the city, but ultimately he would see the destruction of everything he had worked to achieve. 2 Peter 2:7-8 tells us that his soul was tormented as he lived in those cities and watched the evil around him.

> And if he rescued righteous Lot, greatly distressed by the sensual conduct of the wicked (for as that righteous man lived among them day after day, he was tormenting his righteous soul over their lawless deeds that he saw and heard).

Lot could not be happy apart from the presence of God. His selfish choice was disastrous for him and his family and tormented his "righteous soul."

Notice what Genesis 4:16 tells us about Cain. Leaving the presence of the Lord, Cain "settled" in the land of Nod. The Hebrew word "settled" can be translated by "remain," "inhabit" or "abide." To settle has the sense of putting down roots. There is finality in the word. This would now become Cain's home. This is where he would live and raise his family.

Cain's decision to leave the presence of God and settle in Nod would impact not only him but also the generations to come. Future generations would be separated from the blessing of the Lord and grow up not knowing Jehovah God. It is interesting to note that before continuing the story of Adam and Eve, Genesis 4 traces the line of Cain for five generations to a man by the name of Lamech. Listen to what Genesis 4:23-24 tells us about this man:

> 23 Lamech, said to his wives:
> "Adah and Zillah, hear my voice;
> you wives of Lamech , listen to what I say:
> I have killed a man for wounding me,
> a young man for striking me,
> 24 if Cain's revenge is sevenfold,
> then Lamech's is seventy-sevenfold

This account of Lamech is interesting because it shows us how he justified the murder of a young man on the basis of what his ancestor Cain did many years prior. It also shows us the impact that Cain's sin had on generations to come. They too were separated from God and His ways.

Cain chose to leave the presence of God. As bad as this decision was, his decision to "settle" in Nod was worse. If there is one thing worse than leaving the presence of God it is the decision to "settle" in this state and never return. Cain would die separated from the presence of the Lord and give birth to generations of children who would grow up without knowledge of God and His blessings. What a tragic decision this was.

Notice that Cain settled in the land of Nod. The Hebrew word "Nod" literally means "wandering." Cain settled in the land of "wandering." He made up his mind that this is where he would dwell. He would set down his roots (settle) in a place of wandering. He would wander from the purpose of God. He would wander from the knowledge of God. He would wander from fellowship with God. He would wander from the blessings of God. This is the barren place Cain would call home. This is where he would raise his children. He knew the truth but would have nothing to do with it.

God did not stop Cain. He gave him the freedom of choice in this matter. Cain would, of his own free will, choose to settle in the land of Nod (the land of wandering). He would live there until he died, never to return to the fullness of God's blessing on his life and family.

Wandering is not just the sin of the unbeliever. Even believers can be guilty of this sin. Any time we chose to walk in disobedience, we wander from the fullness of God's presence. The church of Laodicea in Revelation 2 was guilty of losing her first love. She had wandered from God. Churches can lose their focus. Believers can lose their joy. We can wander from our calling and lose sight of the purpose of God for our lives. Even believers can become settled in the land of Nod.

Nod is a place of rebellion and wandering; a place of compromise and pride, far from the fullness of God's blessing. To live in the presence of God requires a submission to the Lord and His purpose for our lives. Not everyone is willing to make this commitment.

We ask ourselves: What would make someone leave the presence of the Lord, to "settle" in the city of Nod? We know, however, the temptation in our own heart and the pull of the flesh. Ultimately it is our pride that entices us to leave the fullness of God's presence. The prodigal son would return to his father. Lot would be set free from the torment of the cities of Sodom and Gomorrah, but Cain would choose to "settle" in his wandering. How about you?

For Consideration:

- What is the difference between Lot, the prodigal son and Cain?
- What does the word "settled" imply in Genesis 4:16? What does this teach us about Cain's attitude and decision? Have you ever met people who have the same attitude as Cain?
- What was the impact of Cain's decision on future generations? How do our decisions impact our children and generations to come?
- What does "Nod" mean. What does this teach us about Cain's decision?
- What keeps us in a place of wandering and separation from God?

For Prayer:

- Do you find yourself wandering from God today? Ask the Lord to give you grace to turn from your wanderings and be restored to Him.

- Ask God to forgive you for your wandering. Ask Him to enable you to have a more positive impact on the generations to come.
- Ask God to open your heart to see any areas in your life that are not in submission to Him.
- Thank the Lord that the door is open for us to come into His presence and experience the fullness of His blessings.

6

E AST OF E DEN

Then Cain went away from the presence of the Lord and settled in the land of Nod, east of Eden (Genesis 4:16)

In this study we have seen how Cain chose to leave the presence of the Lord and settle in the land of Nod. There is one more detail we need to see in this verse. Notice that Nod was "east of Eden."

Eden was the land where God had placed Adam and Eve. It was here that they lived in harmony and intimacy with God and His purpose for their lives. In the Garden of Eden, Cain and his parents had experienced the fullness of God's purpose until sin destroyed their fellowship.

The word "Eden" in the Hebrew language means "pleasure." God placed Adam, Eve and their children in the Garden of Pleasure and Delight. There is something very incredible about this. By placing Adam and Eve in "Eden," God was showing them His purpose for their lives. God wanted to bless them and fill them with delight and satisfaction. He filled their lives with good things and chose to enter a deep and intimate relationship with them. There could be no greater satisfaction and fulfillment for them.

Why would God desire to put Adam and Eve in the Garden of Eden (pleasure)? What would motivate a holy God to satisfy His creatures with such joys? Why would He choose to love and delight them?

God is under no obligation to us. He is a great and holy God who deserves our worship and obedience. He is a sovereign Lord and King. This, however, is what makes Eden so incredible. Eden is God's gift to an undeserving people. It is the gracious gift of a holy God to His creatures. It is an unmerited token of His love and devotion to us as His people.

Though undeserved, Eden is God's desire for His people. He longs to satisfy the deepest desire of your heart. He longs to become the greatest delight and pleasure you can ever know. His desire from the beginning of time was that we live in the Garden of Delight and Pleasure, experiencing the fullness He has for us. He longs to fill us, and knows exactly what will bring us the greatest pleasure and delight.

God gives us many wonderful things in this world in which we can take delight. To limit pleasure to the things of this world, however, is to seriously misunderstand the fullness and satisfaction God wants to bring. He can fill us with more delight than anything this world could ever give. Our greatest pleasures will not be in what this world gives but in our Creator. Only He can satisfy the true longing of our soul.

Cain settled east of Eden. He chose to live outside the fullness of God's pleasure and fullness. He settled for something less than what God intended. How about you? Have you become content with something far less than God's best? Have you been living on the outskirts of Eden?

We do not deserve the fullness God wants to give. I know who I am as a sinner and understand that I have not measured up to God's standard. I fail in my walk with God, saying and doing things that displease Him. Were it not for His forgiveness and grace, I would have no hope. Yes, I am undeserving of God's fullness. The reality of the matter, however, is that God created me to enjoy Him and find full delight and satisfaction in Him. As undeserving as I am, this is still God's heart for me. I dare not add to my rebellion, the sin of refusing to enter into this fullness.

To refuse the fullness of Eden is to be content with far less than He intends. It is also to sin against His purpose for I will never reach my potential as His servant if I do not learn to live in the fullness of His blessing and enabling.

It was sin that drew Cain from the presence of the Lord. Through His Son Jesus Christ, however, God has removed the obstacle of sin so that we can once again experience fellowship and delight in Him forever. God felt so strongly about this matter that He willingly sacrificed His only Son so that we could be restored.

Sin in our lives is a hindrance to the fullness of delight God intends. God still offers us the privilege of experiencing the delights of Eden. Speaking to the people of His day the Lord Jesus said:

> … If anyone thirsts, let him come to me and drink, whoever believes in me, as the Scripture has said, "Out of his heart will flow rivers of living water." (John 7:37-38)

Jesus would go on to say in John 10:10:

> The thief comes only to steal and kill and destroy, I came that they may have life and have it abundantly.

Notice what Jesus says in these verses. When we come to Him and believe, He creates rivers of living water in our hearts. These are refreshing and joy-giving waters satisfying the deepest thirst of our soul. He reminds us that He came to this earth so that we could experience abundant life. Are we experiencing these rivers of living water today? Are we delighting in the abundant life Jesus came to give?

It is quite easy to see the delight of Paul in his relationship with the Lord when He said in Philippians 1:21: "For to me to live is Christ, and to die is gain." The greatest delight of Paul was his relationship with the Lord Jesus. To leave this life and everything it had to offer was to enter the arms of the one He loved and longed for.

No matter what happened to him in life, the apostle Paul knew the presence and delight of God. Writing in Philippians 4:13 he said: "I can do all things through him who strengthens me." Paul faced great obstacles in this life. He suffered more than any other apostle and was persecuted for his faith in the Lord Jesus. In all these things, Paul experienced the abundant strength of the Lord to carry Him through.

What a delight it is to know this enabling of God in our lives and ministry. This does not mean that everything will be easy for us. I have often found that God's strength and fellowship is most felt in the struggles and trials of life. Often it is in the place of weakness that we experience the greatest strength and comfort.

The greatest pleasures of Eden come in fellowship with our Creator who walks in this garden with us. Through Jesus we can still delight in the pleasures of the garden. God longs to restore all the blessings sin has stripped from us. He delights in restoring us to fellowship and intimacy. He will give us all we need to experience the fullness of His purpose for our lives.

The question we need to ask ourselves is this: "Are we experiencing the delights of Eden today?" Are we walking in the intimacy God desires for us? We were created for Eden. We were created for pleasure in God and His purpose. Have we settled for something less?

For Consideration:

- What does the word "Eden" mean? What does this teach us about the purpose of God for our lives?
- What keeps us from experiencing the delights of Eden today?
- Do we deserve that God should seek to satisfy us and fill us with His pleasure? Is it a sin for us not to enter the fullness of God's purpose?

- Why have we become content to settle in Nod and not experience the fullness of the pleasures of Eden?
- Have you experienced the fullness of God's purpose for your life? What needs to happen for you enjoy that fullness to a greater extent?
- Should we expect struggle, disappointment and grief in this world? Can we know the delight and joy of God in those times?

For Prayer:

- What satisfaction do you experience in Christ today? Take a moment to thank the Lord for the joy and delight He brings.
- Ask the Lord to show you if there is any part of your life where His delight and pleasure is not found. Ask Him to teach you to rejoice in Him in this area of your life.
- Thank the Lord that even as we live in this world of sin, we can still experience the delights of Eden. Ask God to help you to experience more of Eden's delights as you grow in your walk with Him.

7

LIVING IN THE FULLNESS OF EDEN

In this final chapter, I want to examine what we have learned from Genesis 4:16 about living in the fullness of God's purpose. We could write an entire book on the subject. This, however, is a study of Genesis 4:16 and so my goal is to see what this particular verse has to teach us in this regard. Let's conclude by taking a moment to summarize what this verse and its context teaches.

WE WERE CREATED FOR EDEN

The first thing we learn from the context of Genesis 4:16 is that God created us to live in the fullness of Eden. God placed Adam and Eve in the Garden of Eden to experience its pleasures, blessings and privileges. Sin stripped them of the fullness of those privileges but through the work of the Lord Jesus we can still experience Eden's pleasures in our lives today. Scripture speaks of many of these blessings.

Paul speaks to the Philippians about a peace that surpasses all understanding in Philippians 4:7. James tells us that the Lord God will fill us with His wisdom if we ask (James 1:5). Paul declared that he could do all things through the strength of Christ in him (Philippians 4:13). Jesus promised that those who believed in Him would experience rivers of living water welling up within them (John 7:38). Jesus reminded His listeners that the Father was glorified when they produced much fruit in their lives (John 15:8). He also promised that if we asked anything in His name He would do it (John 14:14). These are a few of the many verses that speak about some of the blessings of Eden we can experience in this world. Jesus came to restore these blessings to us. He laid down His life so that we could know this fullness of pleasure as we walk each day in His presence.

If we are to experience the fullness of Eden today, we must first remember that we were created to live in Eden and our greatest pleasure and joy in life will be found in the presence of God and under His blessings. We must also accept that this is the purpose of God for us. He created us to live in Eden and when that was stripped from us by sin, He sent His Son to die so that those blessings could be restored. We are unworthy of these great privileges, but God delights in us and desires to fill and empower us for His glory, our pleasure and the expansion of His kingdom.

WE ARE GOD'S POSSESSION

The second principle we learn from Genesis 4:16 is found in the in the reason His mother called him Cain. Cain was the possession of God. If we are to experience the fullness of Eden we must settle this matter in our minds and wills. We do not belong to ourselves. We were created by God and for God (Romans 11:36). Paul reminds us in 1 Corinthians 6:20 that we were also bought with a price—the death of God's only Son. His death redeemed us from sin and made us children of God. We belong to Him and He is our Lord and Master.

As servants of God, our mission in life is to honour and glorify His name. If we are to experience the fullness of His blessings, we must be willing to die to our own ideas and agendas and surrender fully to Him and His purpose. Until we surrender and accept this fact, we will never be able to experience the fullness of God's blessing in our lives. Only in full surrender can we know the true and full blessings of Eden. He must possess me and all I have. He must have full control over every detail of my life. I will never experience the fullness of Eden if I am not willing to let Him be my Lord and Master.

THE FULL BLESSINGS OF EDEN ARE IN GOD'S PRESENCE ALONE

The third principle we find in Genesis 4:16 about living in the blessings of Eden is found in what happened when Cain left the presence of the Lord. When Cain left the presence of God he also left the fullness of God's blessings. You see, the blessings of Eden can only be found in the presence of God. God is the blessing of Eden. Eden offers no blessings apart from God.

There are many people who want to experience the blessings of God but they are not ready to remain in His presence. To remain in the presence of God is to be confronted by our sinfulness. To remain in His presence requires that we deal with anything that is an affront to God's holiness. Remaining in the presence of God requires submission to His will and purpose. Not everyone is willing to do this. Many want God's blessings but also want to live in the land of Nod away from the presence of the Lord.

You can't leave God behind and experience the blessings of Eden. He is the blessing. It is His peace and joy that fills us. It is His strength and wisdom that guides us. Walk away from God and you walk away from the source of all your blessings. If you want God's blessing you need God.

If you want to know the blessing of God in any aspect of our life, He must be part of that area of your life. He must be given access to our thoughts and our attitudes. He must be in our family, life and work. His presence must be in all we do. We must make it our commitment never to leave the presence of God. Only in His presence can we experience the fullness of Eden's blessings.

WE MUST NOT BE CONTENT IN NOD

Finally, notice that Cain "settled" in the land of Nod (wandering). Cain chose to make Nod his home and he was content to live in the land of wandering. I have met believers who have been content to live in Nod. I'm not saying that they are rebelling against the Lord and His purposes in a defiant way. What I am saying, however, is that they have become content to remain where they are. Their desire to experience Eden's blessings has faded. Their thirst for God and His will has "settled". They have not reached their potential for the Lord or experienced all the Lord has for them but they have somehow become comfortable with where they are. There are spiritual gifts that remain unused. There are frontiers in their spiritual life that have never been explored. There are battles that have never been fought and victories yet to be obtained. They seem content to live in the shadows of Eden tasting only a portion of God's fullness. They look forward to fullness in the life to come but experience very little Eden's present joys. Their delight in past glories of days lived in Eden seems to satisfy them.

Nod is a temptation for us all. To settle "east of Eden" seems comfortable. It removes us from the convicting presence of God. It removes us from the challenges of stepping out into the unknown. Nod, however, is a stagnant river. It is a place where years pile up in an ever deepening pool of wasted gifts and opportunities. God calls us today to open our heart to Him afresh. Don't let your heart settle in Nod. Don't become comfortable in compromise.

Cry out to God today and say: "Lord, I long for your presence in my life. I never want to leave that presence." How many believers live their lives outside of this blessed presence? They live without seeking God's presence and fullness. They have settled for an existence in Nod full of untapped potential and blessing. God and the reality of his power are distant. God is a theology to be learned and not a person to enjoy. The Christian life is a series of rules and not the response of a grateful heart. Victory is a potential but never really a reality. This is the life East of Eden. Only in the presence of God are these blessings a reality.

May God give us grace to resist the temptation to settle for Nod when we were created and redeemed through the death of His Son to experience the blessings and fullness of Eden.

For Consideration:

- What evidence is there in Scripture that we were created to live in the blessings of Eden? What are some of the blessings the Lord promises those who belong to Him?
- What does it mean to live as God's possession? How does living in surrender to God open the door for us to experience the fullness of God's blessings?
- Can we experience the fullness of God's blessings outside of His presence?
- How do we make God part of all we do?
- Have you become content with something less than God's fullness in your life? Are you aware of His presence in what you do? Explain.

For Prayer:

- Take a moment to thank the Lord for the way He desires to fill us and use us for His glory.
- Ask God to give you grace to surrender more fully to Him and His purpose for your life. Ask Him to reveal any areas of your life that are not surrendered to Him.
- Ask God to be in all you do. Ask Him to be part of your thoughts, attitudes and activities.
- Ask God to give you a deeper passion to become all He wants you to be. Surrender your life afresh to Him to use as He sees fit.

Light To My Path Book Distribution

Light To My Path (LTMP) is a book writing and distribution ministry reaching out to needy Christian workers in Asia, Latin America, and Africa. Many Christian workers in developing countries do not have the resources necessary to obtain Bible training or purchase Bible study materials for their ministries and personal encouragement. F. Wayne Mac Leod is a member of Action International Ministries and has been writing these books with a goal to distribute them to needy pastors and Christian workers around the world.

To date thousands of books are being used in preaching, teaching, evangelism and encouragement of local believers in over sixty countries. Books have now been translated into a number of languages. The goal is to make them available to as many believers as possible.

The ministry of LTMP is a faith based ministry and we trust the Lord for the resources necessary to distribute the books for the encouragement and strengthening of believers around the world. Would you pray that the Lord would open doors for the translation and further distribution of these books?

For more information about Light To My Path Book Distribution visit our website at www.ltmp.ca.

Printed in Great Britain
by Amazon

85394367R00031